"spend your

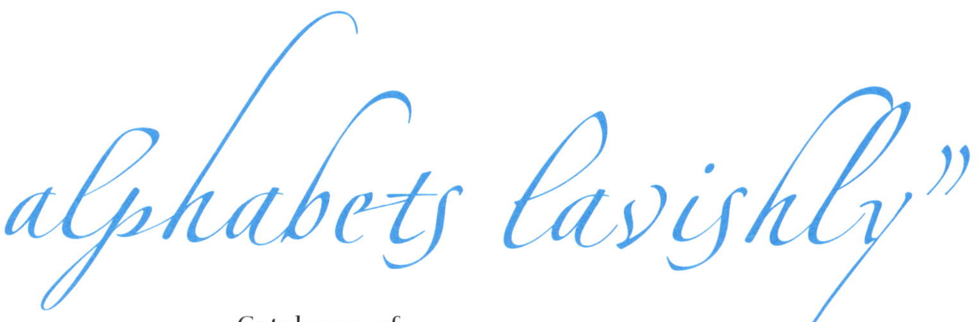

Catalogue of

an exhibition at

the Melbert B. Cary, Jr. Graphic Arts Collection

Rochester Institute of Technology

by Jerry Kelly

with an introduction by David Pankow

RIT CARY GRAPHIC ARTS PRESS

ROCHESTER 2007

The title for this catalogue was taken from *Les Miserablés* by Victor Hugo.

Introduction

The Cary Graphic Arts Collection is privileged to present a survey of work by Hermann and Gudrun Zapf. Coinciding with the formal opening of a new publishing facility for the Cary Graphic Arts Press, this exhibition is dedicated to these remarkable individuals and honors a fifty-year-long relationship with RIT. Many of the extraordinary examples of calligraphy, type design, book design, and bookbinding displayed here have not been on public view before and are drawn entirely from the Zapf archives at RIT.

The university's connection to the Zapf's began with a visit by Hermann to RIT's original downtown Rochester campus in 1957. Over the next twenty years Hermann developed a close friendship with Alexander S. Lawson, a professor in the School of Printing and a noted authority on type history. In 1969, with Lawson's enthusiastic encouragement, RIT acquired the Cary Graphic Arts Collection, a rare book library devoted to the history of the book and printing. Blessed with strong holdings in German type and book design, this remarkable collection's first curator was Alex Lawson. One of his first acts was to establish a distinguished award series named in honor of the American type designer Frederic W. Goudy. The first recipient of the Goudy Award was Hermann Zapf; eight years later, in 1977, he was appointed to succeed Lawson as Cary Professor.

Though Hermann Zapf's active teaching career at RIT spanned only a decade (1977–78 as Cary Professor, followed by nine years as a visiting professor), Hermann's influence on the Institute's printing and design programs was profound and wide-reaching. His classes included students from the School of Printing, but also, and more significantly, those classes came to attract an extraordinary group of calligraphers, type designers, and book designers from all over the world. His two-week summer calligraphy sessions, along with the collegial dinners and parties that followed each day's session, became legendary experiences for those who found their way to western New York. No teacher could have been more selfless with his time.

During his tenure as Cary Professor, Hermann Zapf made extensive use of the Cary Collection. Under Lawson's initial direction, the Cary Collection had developed into an important resource for the students of the School, an intimate place where type specimens and landmark examples of historic printing were readily at hand for class visits. Hermann came to know the collection well and taught his students the importance of examining original manuscripts and early books. Far from praising his own incredible skills as a calligrapher, he pointed with awe to the pages of writing in a thirteenth-century Bible or to the decoration in a fifteenth-century Book of Hours and declared that their anonymous scribes and rubricators were the true craftsmen, individuals whose finely tuned skills with quill pen and simple inks were the envy of modern practitioners of the calligraphic art. Likewise, Hermann made his students look at the early types of Jenson, Aldus, Arrighi, and Garamond. He spoke intimately of Caslon, Baskerville, and Bodoni, as well as of Morris, Johnston, Goudy, Koch, Trump, and countless other designers, whose work he had studied until the subtle forms and proportions of their types and letterforms were revealed to him. He spoke of his own types as well, fascinating his classes with their histories and antecedents; he showed how some were rooted in classic inscriptions, while others took their inspiration from lettering and calligraphic exercises he had made since youth. This was teaching at its best: intimate and attentive, master and students engaged in the landscape of learning.

From the beginning, Hermann took great interest in improving the holdings of the Cary Collection. On one occasion, he learned that the specimen album of Charles Derriey was available, and urged that it be purchased for the library. Published in Paris in 1862, this extravagantly produced volume of decorative types, borders, and calligraphic flourishes is one of the rarest and most beautiful of all nineteenth-century type specimens. This masterpiece of type, composition, and color printing also had a distinguished provenance, since it had once belonged to the well-known typographic authority Jackson Burke. Though the book came with an expensive price tag, Hermann insisted that its acquisition was vital, if the Cary Collection aspired to become a great center for type studies and printing. The purchase was made, and today, 30 years later, the Derriey specimen forms one of the cornerstones of a type specimen collection of international reputation.

In 1991, RIT presented Gudrun Zapf von Hesse with the Goudy Award, recognizing her own considerable achievements in bookbinding, calligraphy, and type design. It was an honor long overdue and came to have special meaning for the Cary Collection since the award event was planned in conjunction with the dedication that year of a new and enlarged facility for the library. In her acceptance talk, Gudrun spoke of her ancestral connections to the famous Luther type foundry in Frankfurt, her early training in bookbinding, and her conviction that a mastery of calligraphy was essential to becoming a good type designer. The "human touch," she said, should never be sacrificed, no matter how advanced the type designer's tools become. Indeed, all of her typefaces, including the slim and beautiful Diotima, elegant Carmina, graceful Columbine, sturdy Alcuin, and energetic Nofret come from the hand of a calligrapher steeped in the history and practice of letterforms. Look carefully at the type used to set this catalog – it is Nofret.

Over the years, Hermann and Gudrun Zapf have generously supported RIT and the Cary Collection, helping us, for example, to acquire a magnificent collection of books and correspondence assembled by Paul Standard, as well as making generous gifts of material from their own archives. Today, the library houses the best collection of Zapf material in any institution outside of Germany, and includes, among many other treasures, original calligraphy for Hermann's *Feder und Stichel*, the layouts and proofs for the two editions of his Manuales and the *Orbis Typographicus*, as well as exquisite bindings and exemplars of calligraphy by Gudrun Zapf.

On the fiftieth anniversary of his first visit to RIT, Hermann recently completed a monumental project, namely the design of a glass wall – formed of 27 eight-foot-high transparent glass panels – that spirals around a new publishing facility for the Cary Graphic Arts Press. Sandblasted on the surface of the panels is a tightly woven narrative of 30 carefully selected quotations from prominent authors and designers about the alphabet, books, reading, and typography, each in a different typeface. Named in honor of Hermann's good friend Alex Lawson, the new facility will declare through its very structure and decoration the fundamental principles of good book design, and will serve as an inspiration for the books that will be conceived and planned within.

When all is said and done, the lives of Hermann and Gudrun Zapf are indelibly recorded in their many contributions to typography and the book arts. The Cary Collection recognizes its obligation to share the treasures in its custody and make them available for study to students and designers. Time will not render irrelevant the simple beauty of Hermann's pencil layouts for the Manuales, or dim the luster of Gudrun's bookbindings. However much new technologies of communication challenge our paradigms of the book and however many new trends come and go, their work will remain beautiful and fresh forever.

David Pankow, *Curator, Cary Graphic Arts Collection*

Catalogue

1– Manuscript trial page for *Die Schicksal,* c. 1937.

Between 1936 and 1948 Zapf completed 52 manuscript books, as well as numerous calligraphic broadsides and several professional commissions for lettering for reproduction, the latter mainly in association with the studio of Paul Koch, Rudolf Koch's son. This is a trial page for one of those works, written in a humanist minuscule that shows the influence of Rudolf Koch's Antiqua typeface (in these early years Koch was a major inspiration for Zapf, an auto-didact who learned from the manuals of Koch and Edward Johnston). This sheet also includes a line in Greek.

2– Trial page in uncial letters for *Feder und Stichel,* c. 1940.

Between 1939 and 1941 Zapf worked on the calligraphy for a book of specimen alphabets and texts, *Feder und Stichel.* The designs were then meticulously cut in metal by August Rosenberger (head punchcutter at the Stempel type foundry) during the war. This layout in uncial letters with a text by the industrial designer Peter Behrens (who designed sever-al typefaces for Stempel in the 1920s) was not used in the published book, but another page in uncial with text by Rudolf Koch appears as plate 5. That page has mostly sim-ilar letterforms, and even a related swash d, f and j, but other characters, such as the e, are noticeably different.

3– Trial page in fraktur for *Feder und Stichel*, c. 1940.

This design, with its large decorative initial L, did not appear in the printed edition of *Feder und Stichel*. As with many of Zapf's works, the final publication is the result of innumerable trials and refinements, revealing the often deceptively simple – and apparently inevitable – final result.

4– Hermann Zapf, *Feder und Stichel*. D. Stempel AG, Frankfurt am Main, 1949.

Feder und Stichel was printed at the house printing office of the Stempel type foundry in a limited edition of 80 copies in 1949. Subsequently, the plates were reprinted in 1950 (500 copies) and 1952 (500 more copies in German and 2,000 copies of an English edition called *Pen and Graver*). This volume is the first use of Zapf's seminal roman typeface, Palatino (see 26 and 27). The binding for all editions was produced in the workshop of Gudrun von Hesse, an accomplished calligrapher, type designer, & bookbinder who would marry Hermann Zapf in 1951. Her work is displayed in items 30–35.

5– Friedrich Hölderlin, *Griechenland*, 1939.

Manuscript no.20 by Hermann Zapf; finished 5 February 1939. A few of the 52 manuscript books written by Zapf between 1936 & 1948 were written in gold on Japanese paper dyed a deep brownish–purple. The dying process sized the sheet, making it possible to write with ink on the otherwise absorbent Japanese paper. The same technique was later used for several calligraphic broadsides, notably two Shakespeare sonnets. One is now in the Newberry Library in Chicago; the other is in the Philip Hofer collection at Harvard University.

6– Alphabet design, c. 1940.

Zapf developed many lettering styles for his various calligraphic works during the 1930s, '40s and '50s. A humanist cursive is shown in this example, with alternate forms for the majuscule A (5 variants), B, E, F, and R.

7– Metal engraving for Ex Libris: Dr. Hans Schubert, 1948.

The years immediately following the war were extremely difficult for Zapf and most Germans. In order to supplement their income, Zapf and August Rosenberger (the punchcutter at Stempel who collaborated with Zapf on many projects, including *Feder und Stichel, Das Blumen ABC*, as well as the Gilgengart and Palatino typefaces) produced bookplates for various clients, such as this one for a medical doctor.

8– Metal engraving for personal greeting card, 1947.

Like the previous item, this commission consists of calligraphy and drawing by Zapf, cut in metal by August Rosenberger. This design was used as a personal greeting card in 1947. The text reads "And nevertheless, flowers will bloom," reflecting an unbreakable optimism, despite the poor conditions of the period immediately following the war. The drawing, illustrating flowers blooming despite the snow blowing around them and piling up at the roots, graphically reinforces the sentiment.

9– Trial page for *Manuale Typographicum* [I], 1954.

A major typographic work of the post–war era is Zapf's *Manuale Typographicum*. The first volume, in oblong format, was published by the Stempel type foundry in Frankfurt and Museum Books in New York in 1954. It incorporates 100 typographic arrangements of astonishing inventiveness and vitality, using typefaces produced by Stempel. Each page contains a quotation on typography, drawn from a wide assortment of sources in sixteen languages, as well as a complete alphabet showing, printed only in red and black. Like many of Zapf's works, the project went through many stages of development before achieving its final form. Indeed, the Cary Library has layouts and trial pages for the book in a vertical format, using multiple colors – some of those designs were used in a Stempel calendar in 1954. This layout is in the Mundus typeface designed for Stempel by W. Schwerdtner. In the final published edition of *Manuale Typographicum* there are no pages in the Mundus typeface.

10– Hermann Zapf, *Manuale Typographicum* [I]. D. Stempel AG, Frankfurt am Main; and Museum Books, New York, 1954.

1,000 copies of Zapf's first *Manuale Typographicum* were printed in 1954 at the house printing office of the Stempel type foundry. The binding in quarter vellum was executed by Max Bock. All copies contained a separate pamphlet of the texts translated into German or English.

11– Paste up for *About Alphabets*, 1960.

Paul Bennett, president of of the Typophiles of New York, encouraged Zapf to write the story of his life in the letter arts, to be published as a volume in the Typophiles Chap Book series. Almost all of the books in the series are of uni–

form format, which Zapf followed for his autobiographical volume. He designed the book almost entirely in one size and style of type (Optima 9–point Didot), ingeniously using leading, subtle placement, and other devices to distinguish the headlines, captions, and other matter.

12– Hermann Zapf, *About Alphabets*. The Typophiles, New York, 1960.

In addition to the English edition published by the Typophiles, a German edition was published by the Linotype company in Frankfurt under the title *Über Alphabete*. Both editions were printed by Zapf's long–time collaborator, Ludwig Oehms. Oehms was hired by Zapf for the Stempel printing office shortly after the war. In 1951 Oehms established his own printing plant in Frankfurt, going on to print numerous notable volumes, including Zapf's second *Manuale Typographicum* (1968, see items 19–21 below).

  A revised, updated edition of *About Alphabets* was published by MIT Press in 1970. A new book of autobiographical writing, *Alphabet Stories*, has just been co-published by Linotype and the Cary Graphic Arts Press (see item 28 below).

13– Sketch for the Optima typeface, c. 1950.

Optima is one of the most important typefaces of the twentieth century. Today, almost a half century after its initial release, it continues to be one of the most popular fonts available. The design has its origins in some lettering which Zapf saw in the Santa Croce church in Florence during a trip to Italy in 1950. The slender tapering of the serifless letters appealed to Zapf as the possible basis for a new typeface. The design was fairly well developed by 1952, but it was only in 1958 that the initial type family (consisting of roman, italic, and bold in assorted sizes) was made available. This sketch shows several letters of all three variants, comparing the weights and features of the related designs.

14– Optima nova type specimen. Linotype GmbH, Bad Homburg, 2003.

The method of type production is constantly evolving. While it remained essentially unchanged for several centuries, technology finally caught up with typography in the late nineteenth century. In the twentieth century evolution accelerated at a dizzying pace; within a few decades there were more changes in the manufacture of type than had occurred in the previous 500 years; the predominant method of type composition moved from hot–metal composition to phototype to digital type in a mere four decades. Each technology presents new demands on type design. To accommodate digital type generation, Zapf redesigned the entire Optima type family, also adding many useful variants that were unavailable in metal, such as small caps, oldstyle figures, a lovely titling font, as well as condensed versions and additional weights. In the end, the Optima nova family includes over 40 alphabets.

15– Hermann Zapf, *Typographic Variations*. Georg Kurt Schauer, Frankfurt am Main, 1963; Museum Books, New York, 1964, and Editions Hermann, Paris, 1965.

A major part of Hermann Zapf's design work throughout the 1950s, '60s, and '70s was in the field of book design.

He worked mainly on a freelance basis, designing trade editions for major German publishers such as Carl Hanser, S. Fisher, Suhrkamp, and Cotta. The *Typographic Variations* publication contains re-settings of 78 book and title pages designed by Zapf up to 1963. While most of the layouts are from volumes that Zapf had designed over the previous decade or so, several others were created specifically for this publication.

16–Hermann Zapf, *Kleine Autobiographie in Lettern*, 1956.

Occasionally Zapf produced inserts for graphic arts periodicals such as *Philobiblon, Imprimatur, Motif,* etc. This 16-page insert was printed in red, blue and black at the Stempel printing office for inclusion in *Der Druckspiegel.* It includes showings of Zapf's 45 alphabet designs up to 1956, and a brief autobiographical text about the designer and his typefaces.

17– Letter to Paul Standard, New York, 5 February 1950.

In 1949 Zapf wrote to Paul Standard to try to secure a copy of Standard's book, *Calligraphy's Flowering, Decay & Restauration* (STA, Chicago, 1947). Due to restrictions on sending money out of Germany it was difficult for Zapf to purchase books from overseas. Standard sent the young Hermann Zapf an inscribed complimentary copy; it was the beginning of a friendship that would continue uninterrupted until Standard's death on January 1, 1992. Many of the early letters from Zapf to Standard had exquisite calligraphic headpieces, such as this one.

18– Hermann Zapf, *Calligraphic Salutations*. Cary Graphic Arts Collection, Rochester, NY, 1993.

A selection of some of Zapf's early letters to Paul Standard (which are now in the Cary Collection) are reproduced in their original colors in this 1993 publication. 600 copies were printed at the Stinehour Press, of which 30 are on Arches paper and handbound.

19– Layout sketch for the Galileo page in *Manuale Typographicum* [II], c. 1965.

Almost immediately upon the completion of Zapf's first *Manuale Typographicum* (see nos. 9 & 10 above) he began work on a second volume of 100 typographic arrangements, this time in vertical format, and using typefaces from assorted type foundries, not just Stempel. This page is set in the Bodoni re-cutting made under the direction of the punch-cutter Louis Hoell at the Bauer type foundry in the 1920s. Many consider this the finest re-cutting of Bodoni's original fonts. In this arrangement Zapf uses the Bauer Bodoni Titling variant to dramatic effect.

20– Layout sketch for the Da Vinci page in *Manuale Typographicum* [II], c. 1965.

This page form the second *Manuale* is set in Giovanni Mardersteig's Dante fonts. The complex arrangement was printed on Hahnemuhle mould-made paper by Ludwig Oehms (see item 12).

21– Hermann Zapf, *Manuale Typographicum* [II]. Z-Presse, Frankfurt am Main; and MIT Press, Cambridge, MA, 1968.

The second *Manuale Typographicum* (1968), contains 100 texts about typography in eighteen languages set in the types of various type foundries (including some photocomposition printed from plates). This time Zapf had a vertical format – fourteen years after the first volume in horizontal format. The type was composed in numerous shops around the world, with the typeset pages and plates sent to Frankfurt for printing by Oehms.

22–Layout for the SATOR magic square page, *Orbis Typographicus.*

Philip Metzger (1914–1981) pursued his passion for letterpress printing at night and on weekends while working for a utilities company in Kansas City. His excellent taste in typefaces led him to many European foundries, from which he purchased typefaces by many of the great designers of the twentieth century, including, of course, Hermann and Gudrun Zapf. He built up an enviable repertoire of fine foundry fonts, which Hermann Zapf used for this selection of texts on the arts and sciences. Metzger printed them in his spare time over the course of many years. Many of the arrangements were quite experimental, involving a wide assortment of colors and papers.

23–Hermann Zapf, *Orbis Typographicus.* Crabgrass Press, Kansas City, MO, 1990.

99 copies printed by Philip Metzger at his Crabgrass Press. The 25 printed sheets for *Orbis Typographicus* were enclosed in a specially manufactured plexiglass box, which allowed the leaves to be switched, displaying a different one whenever desired. The box could be hung horizontally or vertically, depending on the page shown.

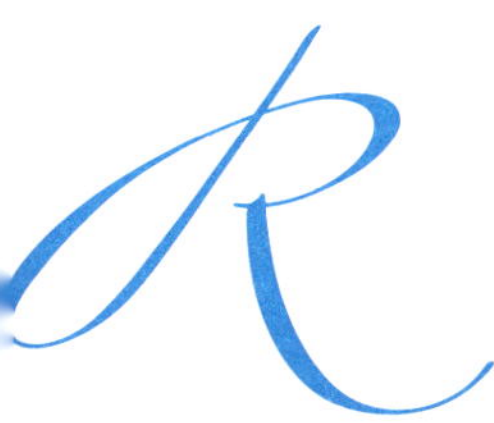

24– Layout for *August Rosenberger.*

In addition to cutting several of Hermann and Gudrun Zapf's typeface designs, August Rosenberger (1893–1980) cut the metal plates for Hermann Zapf's *Feder und Stichel* (1949) and *Das Blumen ABC* (1962), as well as other smaller projects (see items 4, 7 and 8). This tribute volume gives a brief biography of this skilled craftsman, one of the last masters of an exacting art.

25– Hermann Zapf, *August Rosenberger.* Cary Graphic Arts Collection, Rochester, NY, 1996.

The book was handset in Palatino type by Jerry Kelly and David Pankow, and printed by them on a Vandercook proof press at the Cary Collection. 110 copies were printed, all containing original leaves of prints from Rosenberger's engravings. 35 deluxe copies were specially bound and contained additional material.

26– Palatino type specimen. D. Stempel AG, Frankfurt am Main, 1953.

This specimen book was the first to display the complete Palatino type family, comprised of roman, italic & bold and their Linotype counterparts, along with small caps, old style figures, a more delicate book version called Aldus, and its italic and small caps, a narrow version of Aldus, two titling fonts (the heavy weight Sistina and the light Michelangelo), a Greek text font (Heraklit) with a light display titling (Phidias), and swash italic capitals. All except the italic swash capitals have been modified with expanded character sets for digital composition (see no. 27).

27– Palatino nova type specimen. Linotype GmbH, Bad Homburg, 2005.

Palatino proved to be one of the most successful typefaces of all time. It was originally designed by Zapf for foundry and Linotype composition; both metal–type technologies. This presented many limitations that became obsolete with the advent of phototype and digital character generation systems. However, those technologies imposed new requirements on alphabet designs. Palatino was adapted for a variety of typesetting systems, sometimes sympathetically (as when Hermann Zapf himself was given the opportunity to modify the design), but more often carelessly. In the early years of the twenty–first century, Zapf and Linotype worked on developing a definitive version of the Palatino family for today's typesetting technology. The result includes many characters that are slightly modified from the Linotype phototype version, and other forms (such as the Palatino roman & italic Q and f, or the Michelangelo G and ampersand) which have been more radically re–drawn. In addition, an extensive set of Unicode glyphs for type composition in assorted alphabets such as Cyrillic, Greek, etc., have been incorporated into the Palatino nova series.

28– Hermann Zapf, *Alphabet Stories*. Linotype GmbH, Bad Homburg, 2007.

Today, with the Internet, there is a tremendous amount of information available, and also more mis–information than ever before. Many people are unable to discern fact from fallacy, leading to the perpetuation of incorrect statements. In order to "set the record straight," this new autobiographical volume on the life and work of Hermann Zapf was published this year. The English edition, limited to 300 copies distributed in the United States by the Cary Graphic Arts Press, includes a postscript by David Pankow.

29– Glass panel wall for RIT Cary Graphic Arts Press, Alexander S. Lawson Publishing Center, 2007.

Recently, at the beginning of the twenty-first century, Rochester Institute of Technology has established a new university press. To date, several dozen publications have been issued, and the young publishing imprint is now on pace to publish a dozen or so titles each year. The expanded program has necessitated the construction of a new publishing facility, established within the Wallace Library at RIT. The architects have created a wall of glass panels, for which Hermann Zapf has designed a series of texts about books and typography, which are sandblasted on the glass surface by Pike Stained Glass Studios in Rochester.

30– Full leather binding by Gudrun von Hesse for Friedrich Hölderlin's *Hyperion*. Insel Verlag, Leipzig, 1937.

Gudrun von Hesse was best known in the early 1950s as a fine bookbinder. She studied with Otto Dorfner, establishing her own studio in Frankfurt in 1946. At that time she did much work for the Bauer type foundry. Later her studio moved to a space at the Stempel type foundry, where she worked on many of the foundry's publications from the 1950s. This handbound copy of Hölderlin's *Hyperion* shows her skill in working with leather, and her fresh designs for gold tooling.

31– *Das Hohelied Salomos.* Manuscript book written and bound by
Gudrun von Hesse, 1936.

In addition to her exceptional skill in binding, Gudrun
Zapf is a notable calligrapher and type designer. Initially
Gudrun von Hesse was self-taught in calligraphy (she
learned from the same books by Koch and Johnston her
future husband used). In 1941, she began a course of study
with the calligrapher Johannes Boehland in Berlin. This
volume, written in textura style, is one of several manuscript books completed by her in the 1940s and 1950s.

32– Gertrude von Le Fort, *Plus Ultra.* Trajanus Presse, Frankfurt
am Main, 1950.

Gudrun von Hesses's first typeface design was Diotima.
Hermann Zapf had seen a manuscript book written by Gudrun von Hesse at an exhibition in Frankfurt and thought
it might form the basis for a typeface. The management of
the Stempel foundry accepted the suggestion, and Zapf
then had Gudrun von Hesse draw the design at actual size
in 36–point for a trial cutting (a trying task for any designer). Punches were cut by Rosenberger and eventually an
entire range was produced, along with a lovely companion
italic, one of the finest designs of its kind. The first book to
be printed in Diotima was this edition of *Plus Ultra*, published by the Trajanus Presse, an imprint established by
Gotthard de Beauclair at the Stempel foundry. The binding
in quarter–vellum with original paste papers was entirely
designed by Gudrun Zapf and executed at her workshop in
the Stempel building.

33–Full leather binding by Gudrun von Hesse for Charles de Coster's *Tyll Ulenspiegel und Lamm Goedzak*. Eugen Diedrichs Verlag, Jena, 1936.

Another example of Gudrun von Hesse's skill in working with tooled leather binding. This example is in full pigskin with blind tooling.

34–Nofret type specimen. H. Berthold AG, Berlin, 1986.

In the phototype era, the Berthold type foundry produced some of the highest quality typefaces available, but only for use on their system. In addition to adapting classic designs of the past, Berthold commissioned a series of new designs from various letter artists called "Berthold eklusivs." Gudrun Zapf von Hesse's Nofret design is among the most successful of the Berthold original alphabets.

35–Carmina type specimen. Bitstream, Inc., Cambridge, MA, 1987.

Like Berthold in Germany (see item 34), the Bitstream digital type foundry of Cambridge, Massachusetts, also commissioned original typefaces from noted designers. Carmina is a calligraphic alphabet designed by Gudrun Zapf von Hesse. Page 3 in the specimen book for this font shows the hand–lettered roots of this design.

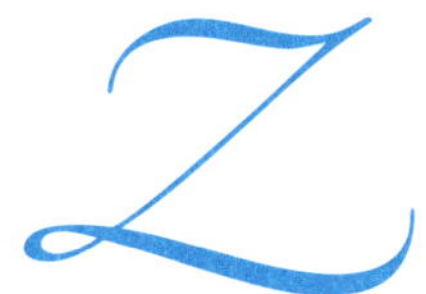

Illustrations

Das Schicksal

Προσκυνουντες την είμαρμενην, σοφοι
ÄSCHYLUS

Als von des Friedens heil'gen Talen,
Wo sich die Liebe Kränze wand,
Hinüber zu den Göttermahlen
Des goldnen Alters Zauber schwand,
Als nun des Schicksals eh'rne Rechte,
Die große Meisterin, die Not,
Dem übermächtigen Geschlechte
Den langen, bittern Kampf gebot:

Da sprang er aus der Mutter Wiege,
Da fand er sie, die schöne Spur
Zu seiner Tugend schwerem Siege,
Der Sohn der heiligen Natur;
Der hohen Geister höchste Gabe,
Der Tugend Löwenkraft, begann
Im Siege, den ein Götterknabe
Den Ungeheuern abgewann.

143

1—Manuscript trial page for *Die Schicksal,* c. 1937.

2–Trial page in uncial letters for *Feder und Stichel,* c. 1940.

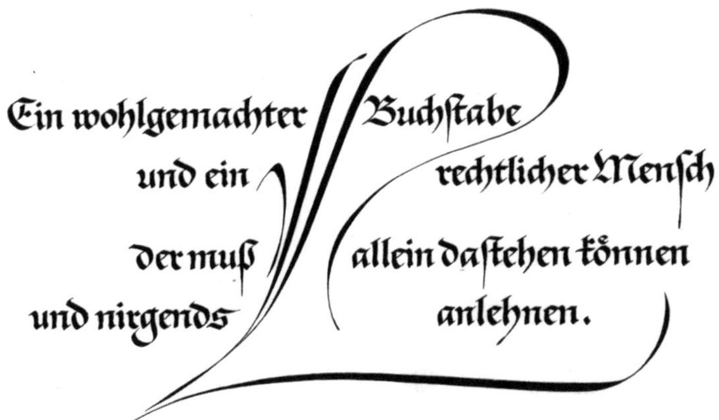

3–Trial page in fraktur for *Feder und Stichel,* c. 1940.

5– Friedrich Hölderlin, *Griechenland*, 1939.

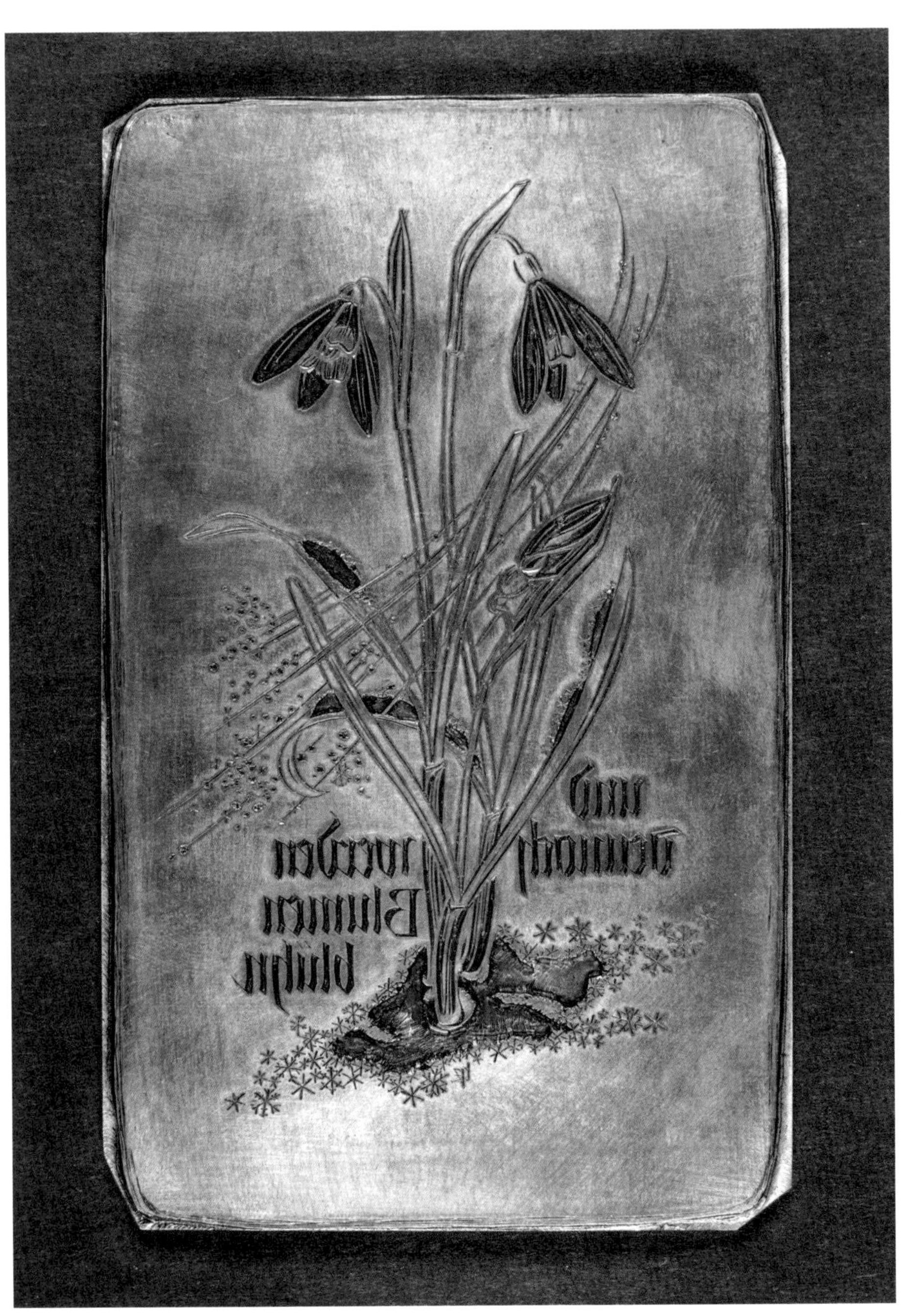

8–Metal engraving for personal greeting card, 1947.

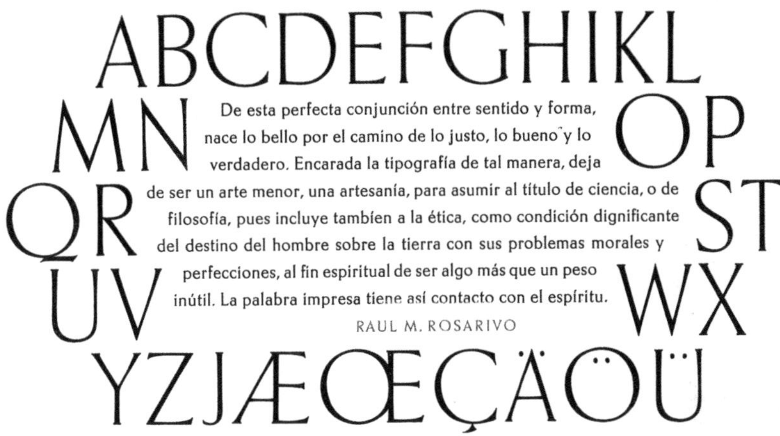

9–Trial page for *Manuale Typographicum* [I], 1954.

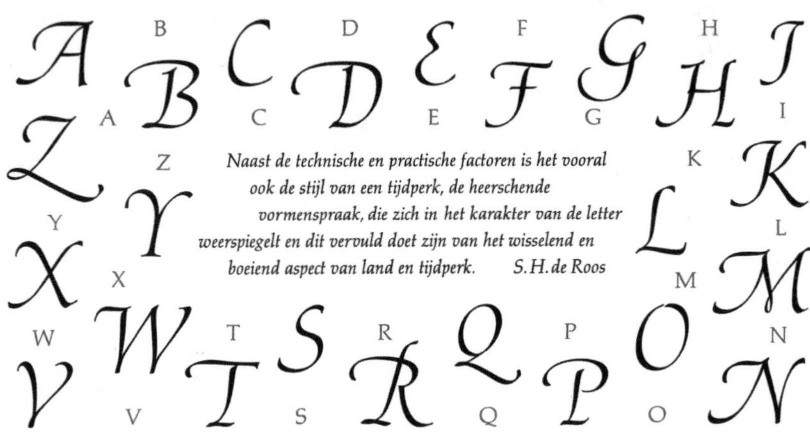

10–Hermann Zapf, *Manuale Typographicum* [I]. D. Stempel AG; and
Museum Books, 1954.

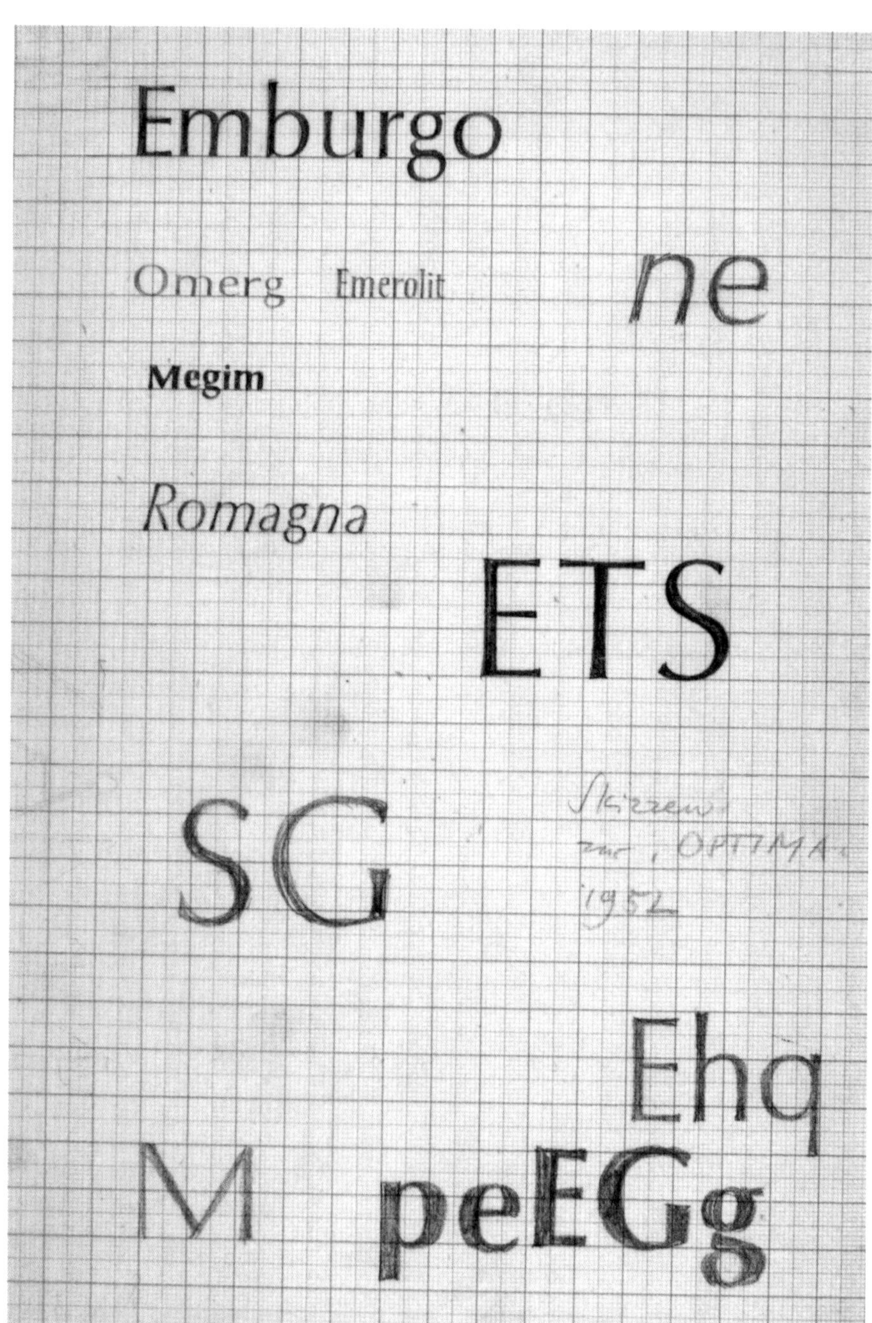

13–Sketch for the Optima typeface, c. 1950.

*Über Aufbau und Gestaltung seiner Druckschriften, die
seit 1938 von der Schriftgießerei D. Stempel AG und der
Linotype GmbH, Frankfurt am Main, herausgegeben
wurden, berichtet auf den folgenden Seiten der Buch-
und Schriftgraphiker Hermann Zapf.* DIE SCHRIFTLEITUNG

KLEINE AUTOBIOGRAPHIE IN LETTERN VON HERMANN ZAPF

TYPOGRAPHIE ist im Grunde zweidimensionale Archi=
tektur. Die Harmonie der einzelnen Proportionen, die
Gruppierung der Schriftzeilen, das Abwägen von Kon=
trast und Ausgleich, die Symmetrie wie die dynamische
Spannung der anaxialen Anordnung sind Gestaltungs=
mittel, die der Typograph je nach der gestellten Auf=
gabe so anzuwenden hat, daß der Text dem Leser in der
ansprechendsten Form vermittelt wird. Seiner Phantasie
sind nur durch die Gesetzmäßigkeit des Materials und
der stilgeschichtlichen Bindungen der Formen Grenzen
gesetzt. Immer wieder ist man erstaunt, welch ein For=
menreichtum den Lettern innewohnt. Es gibt viele herr=
liche Schriften aus den früheren Jahrhunderten, die wir
auch heute noch gern für unsere Druckarbeiten verwen=
den. Vielleicht wird man fragen, warum trotzdem neue
Schriften entworfen werden. Unsere Zeit stellt jedoch
an den Entwerfer andere Aufgaben als die Vergangen=
heit. Eine neue Type muß neben der Schönheit und Les=
barkeit auch den technischen Anforderungen von heute
gerecht werden, wo Schnellpressen und Rotationsma=
schinen an die Stelle der Handpressen, und Maschinen=
papier an die Stelle handgeschöpften Papiers getreten
sind. Ebenso wie unsere Musiker und bildenden Künst=
ler nach einem Ausdruck unserer Zeit suchen und dabei
eine reiche Vergangenheit fortzusetzen haben, so ist die
Arbeit der Schriftentwerfer und der Schriftgießer stets
der großen Tradition des Alphabets verpflichtet.

*Der nebenstehende Text
ist dem Vorwort zum
›Manuale typographicum‹
von Hermann Zapf
entnommen*

›DER DRUCKSPIEGEL‹
*Typographische Beilage
11/1956*

16– Hermann Zapf, *Kleine Autobiographie in Lettern*, 1956.

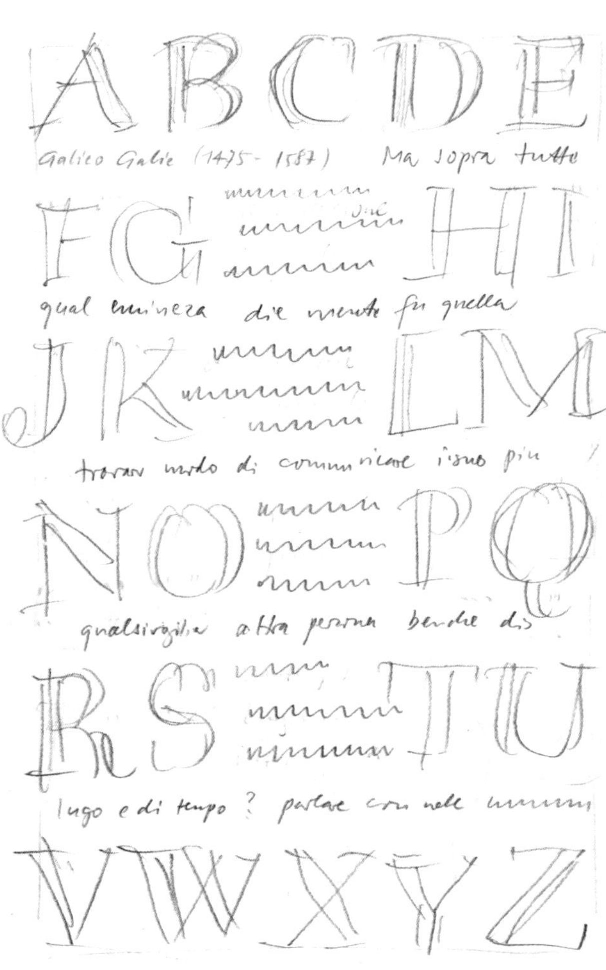

19– Layout for Galileo page for *Manuale Typographicum* [II], c. 1965.

A B C D E

Galileo Galilei Ma sopra tutte le invenzioni stupende, qual

eminenza di mente

fu quella di colui

che s'immaginò

F G   H I

di trovar modo di comunicare i suoi più reconditi pensieri a

qualsivoglia

altra persona, benchè

distante per

J K   L M

lunghissimo intervallo di luogo e di tempo ? parlare con quelli

che son

nell'Indie,

parlare a

N O   P Q

quelli che non sono ancora nati nè saranno se non di

qua a mille

e dieci mila anni ?

e con qual facilità ?

R S   T U

con i vari accozzamenti di venti caratteruzzi sopra una carta.

V W X Y Z

21–Final page set in Bauer Bodoni for *Manuale Typographicum* [II], 1968.

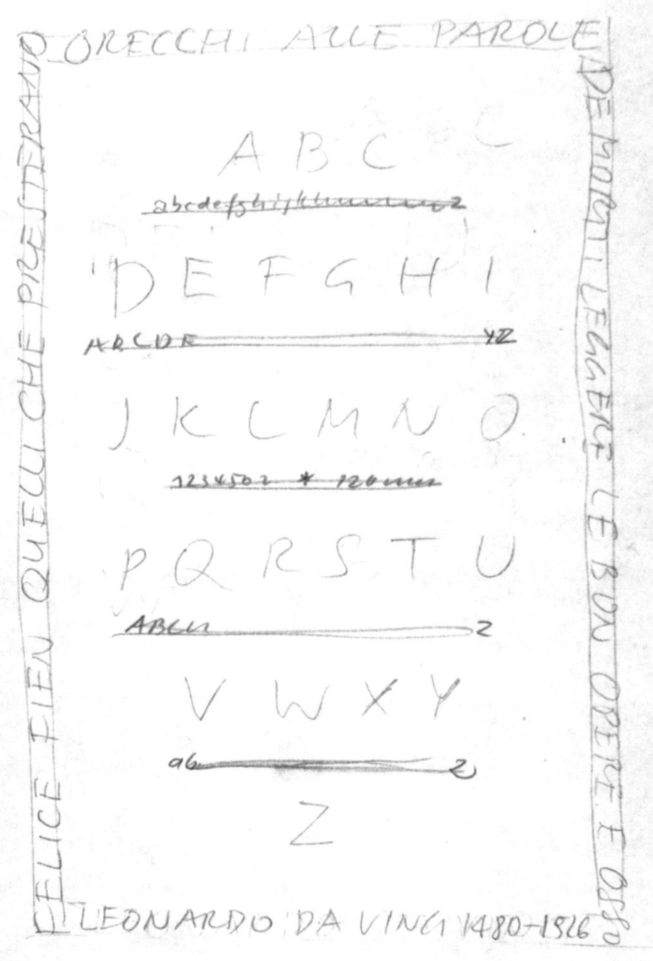

20– Layout sketch for *Manuale Typographicum* [II], c. 1965.

21–Final page set in Dante for *Manuale Typographicum* [II], 1968.

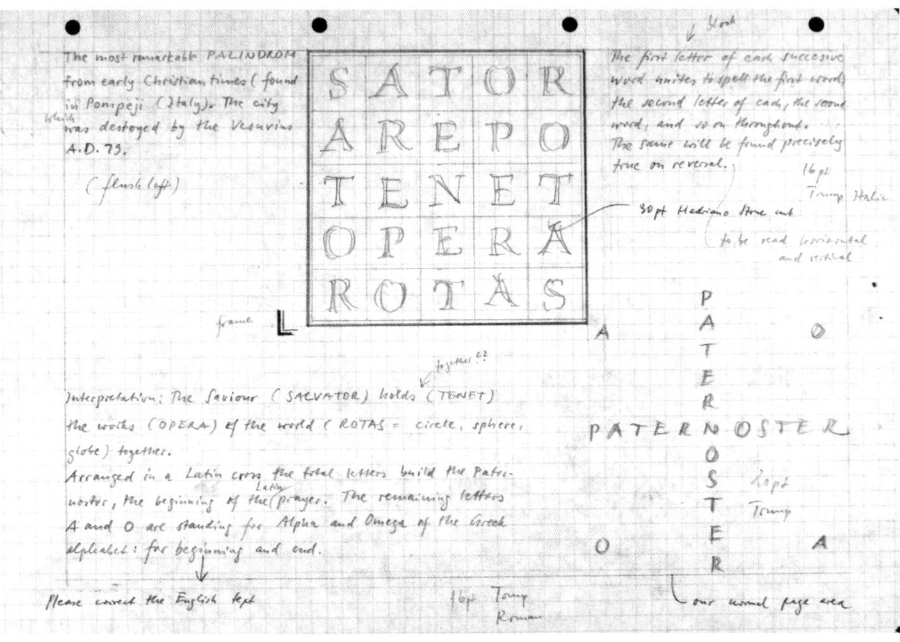

22– Layout for the SATOR magic square page, *Orbis Typographicus*.

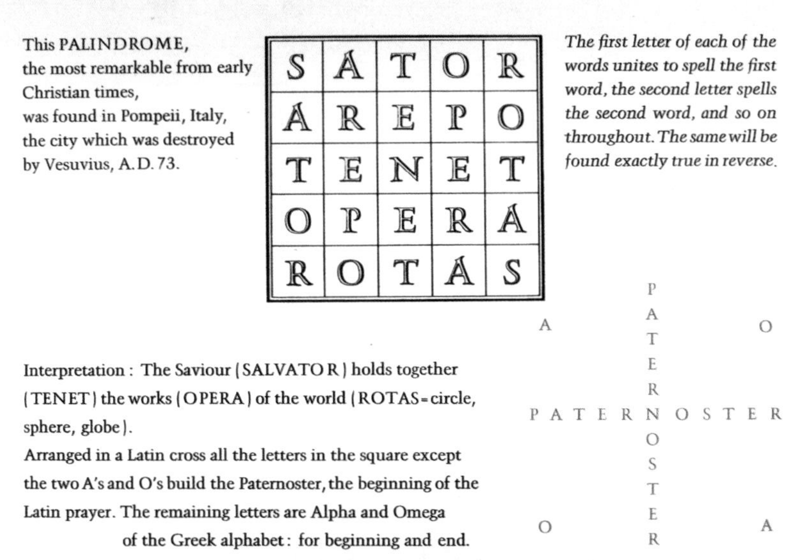

23– Hermann Zapf, *Orbis Typographicus*. Crabgrass Press, 1990.

¶ ABCDEFGHIJKLMNOPQ
RSTUVWXYZ & ÆŒ / Plus accents

Alternative characters
& KRQUWYZ 69O ✣ ✳

€$¢£ƒ¥ 1234567890 €$¢£ƒ¥

[]()[·] ST TH TT NN CO OO · Titling ligatures

@ « » › ‹ ✳ † ‡ § # % ‰ !? ¡¿ .,™©®

ABCDEFGHIJKLMNOPQ Small Caps

RSTUVW & XYZ

Page 17 shows a heavier →
version of this design,
Palatino nova Imperial

€$¢£ƒ¥ O123456789

H 1234567890/12345 1ST 2ND 3RD 4TH TH

∑√ +−±·×÷¬ = ≠ ≈ ~ < > ≤ ≥ ∞ ∫∏

ABΓΔΕΖΗΘΙΚΛΜΝΞΟΠΡΣ
ΤΥΦΧΨΩ

(Phidias Greek to accompany
Palatino nova Titling)

ABΓΔΕΖΗΘΙΚΛΜΝΞΟΠΡΣΤΥΦΧΨΩ Small Caps

GEOMETRY can produce legible letters, but art alone
makes them beautiful. Art begins where geometry ends, and imparts to
letters a character transcending mere measurement. ✣ PAUL STANDARD

27– Palatino nova type specimen, Linotype GmbH, 2005.

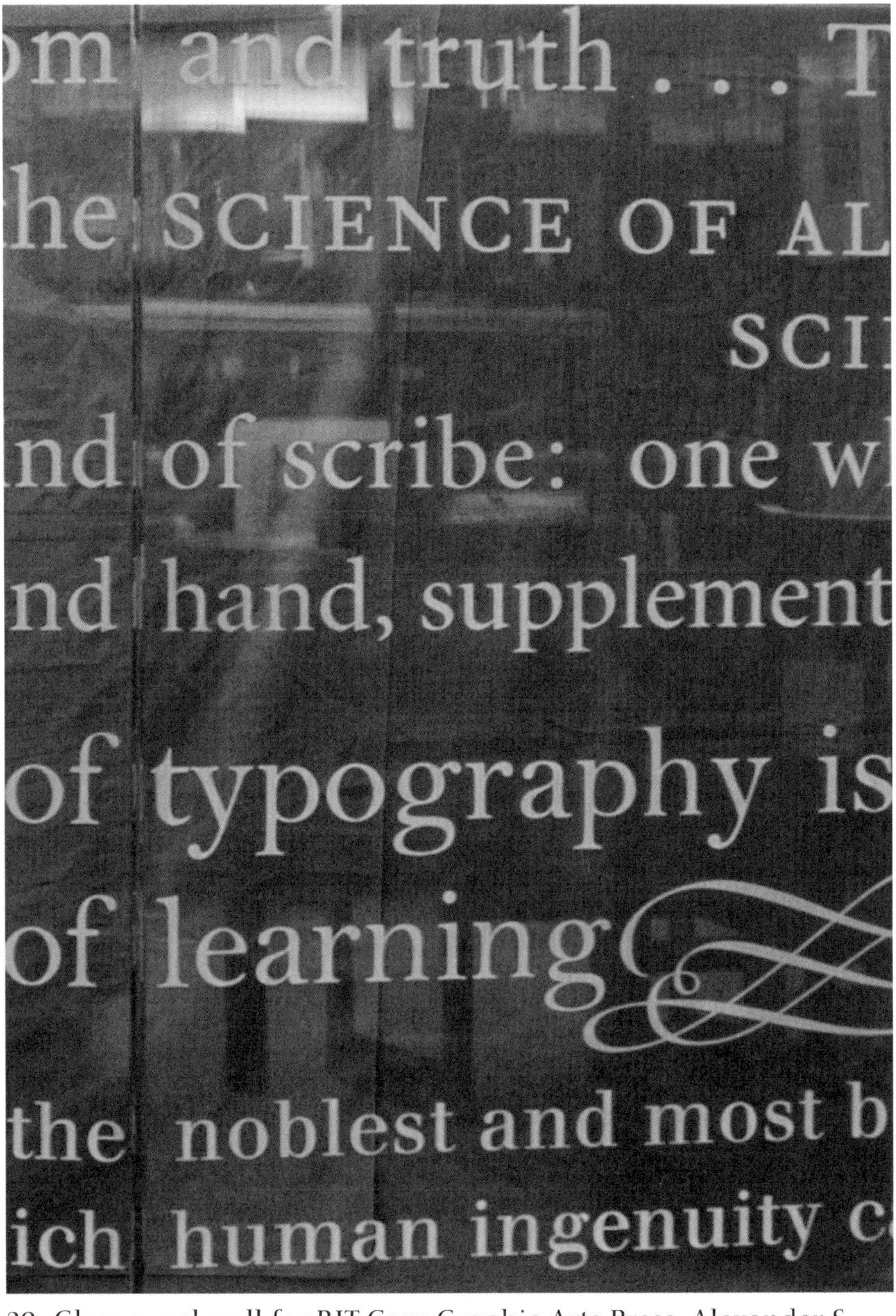

29–Glass panel wall for RIT Cary Graphic Arts Press, Alexander S. Lawson Publishing Center (detail).

1. KAPITEL
Das Hohelied Salomos.

Er küsse mich mit dem Kuß
seines Mundes; denn deine
Liebe ist lieblicher, denn Wein; ¢
Daß man deine gute Salbe rie-
che; dein Name ist eine ausge=
schüttete Salbe, darum lieben
dich die Mägde. ¢ Ziehe mich
dir nach, so laufen wir. Der Kö=
nig führet mich in seine Kam=
mer. Wir freuen uns und sind
fröhlich über dir; wir gedenken
an deine Liebe mehr, denn an den
Wein. Die frommen lieben dich.
¢ Ich bin schwarz, aber gar lieb-
lich, ihr Töchter Jerusalems, wie

31– *Das Hohelied Salomos.* Manuscript book written and bound by
Gudrun von Hesse, 1936.

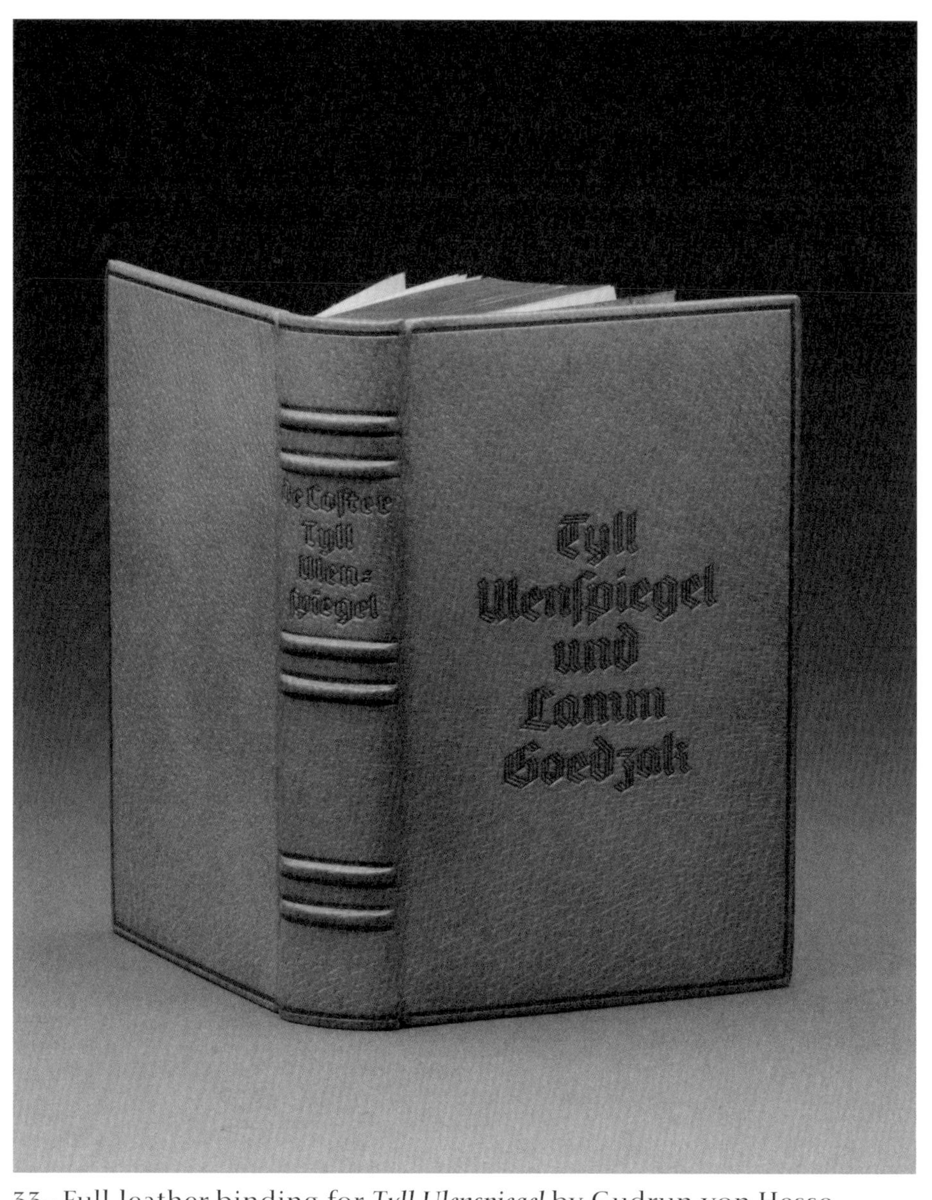

33– Full leather binding for *Tyll Ulenspiegel* by Gudrun von Hesse.

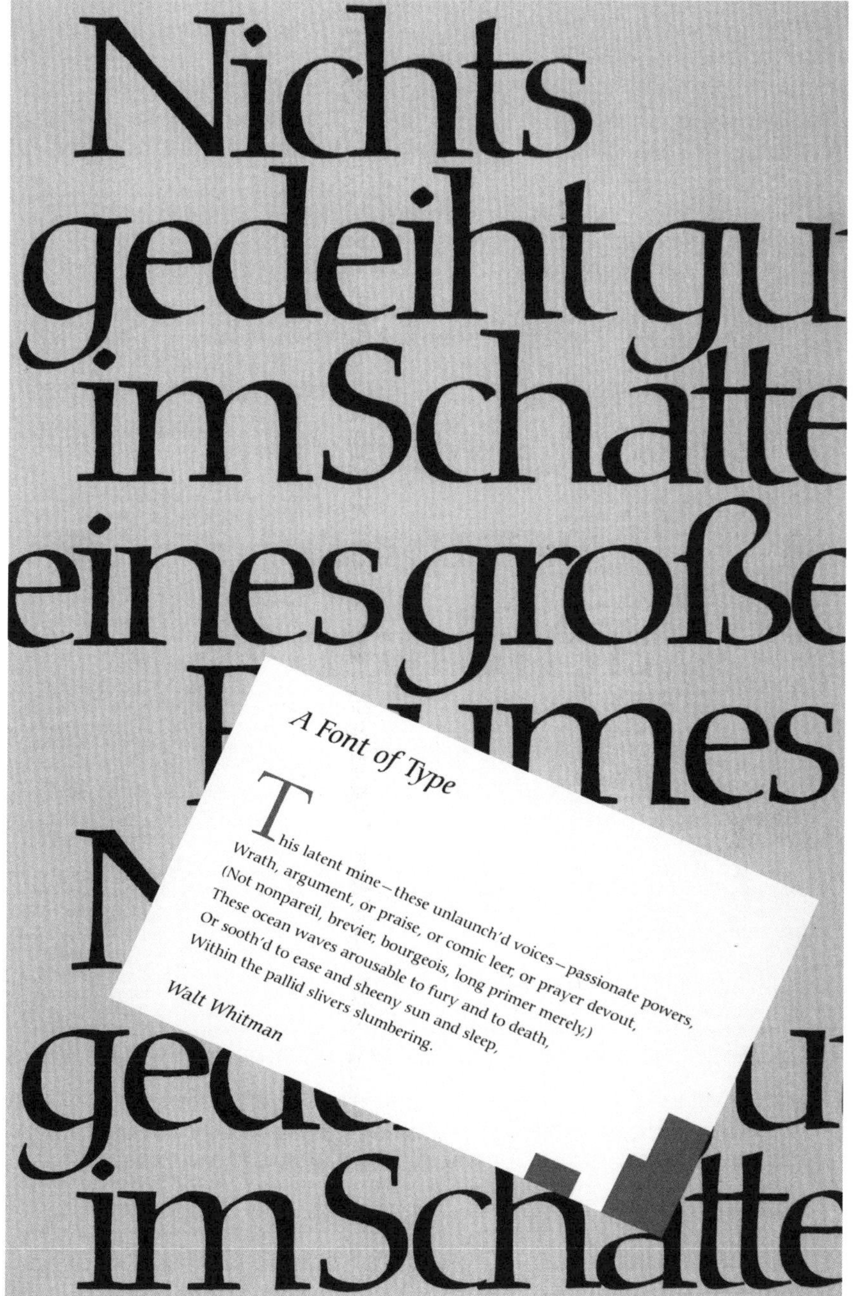

35– Carmina type specimen. Bitstream, Inc., 1989.

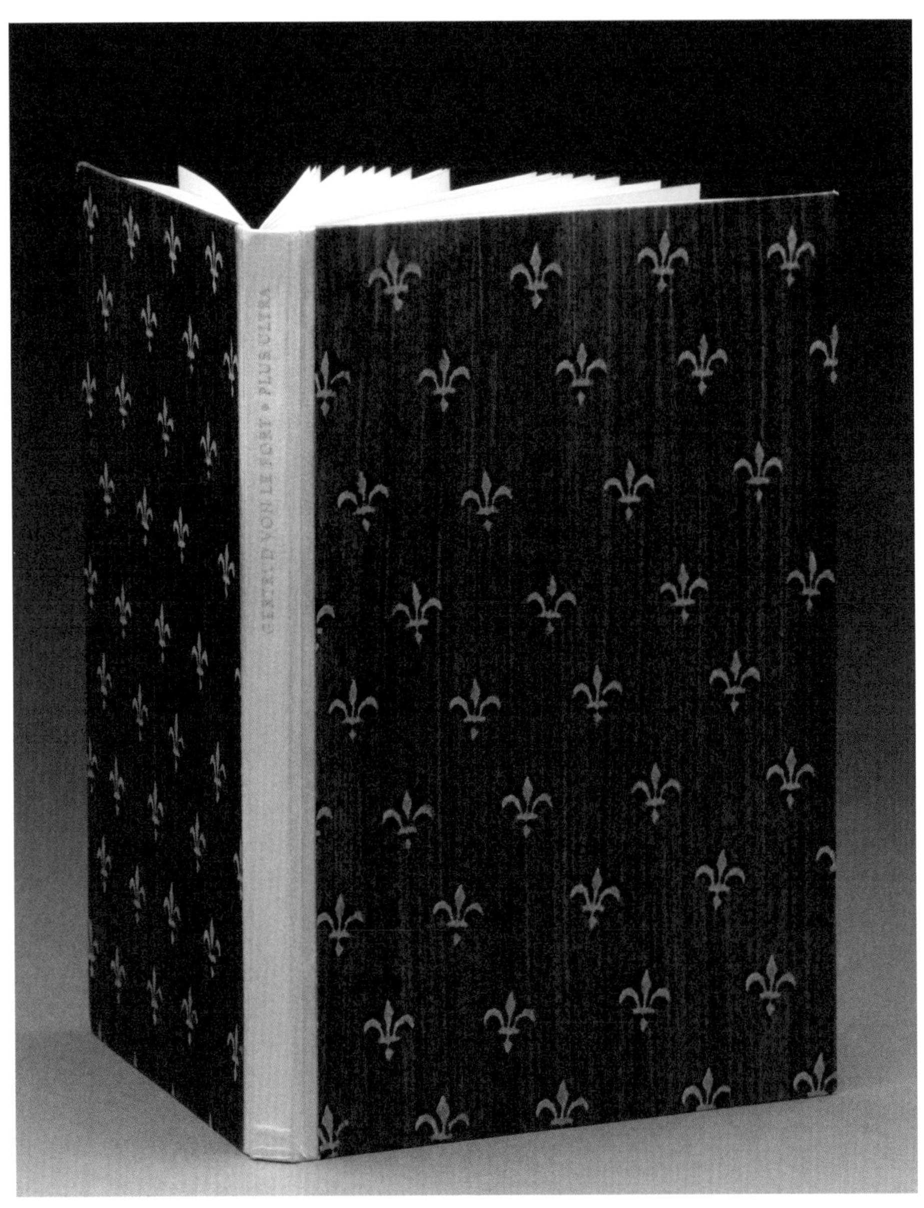

32–Gertrude von Le Fort, *Plus Ultra*. Trajanus Presse, 1950.

Set in 10-point Nofret, designed by Gudrun Zapf von Hesse,

and Linotype Zapfino, designed by Hermann Zapf.

800 copies printed, of which 300 are reserved

for The Typophiles, New York, as New Series Monograph

number 23. Printed on Mohawk paper.

Typography by Jerry Kelly.